STAR TREK™

Starfleet is...

Celebrating the Federation's Ideals

ROBB PEARLMAN

SMART POP

Smart Pop Books
An Imprint of BenBella Books, Inc.
Dallas, TX

Smart Pop is an imprint of BenBella Books, Inc.
10440 N. Central Expressway, Suite 800
Dallas, TX 75231
smartpopbooks.com
benbellabooks.com
Send feedback to feedback@benbellabooks.com

BenBella and *Smart Pop* are federally registered trademarks.

Printed in the United States of America
10 9 8 7 6 5 4 3 2 1

Library of Congress Control Number: 2021012417
9781637740194 (print)
9781637740255 (ebook)

Text design and composition by Aaron Edmiston
Cover design by Brigid Pearson
Cover image © Shutterstock / Vadim Sadovski
Printed by Versa Press

"*Star Trek* was an attempt to say that humanity will reach maturity and wisdom on the day that it begins not just to tolerate but take a special delight in differences in ideas and differences in life forms. [. . .] If we cannot learn to actually enjoy those small differences, to take a positive delight in those small differences between our own kind, here on this planet, then we do not deserve to go out into space and meet the diversity that is almost certainly out there."

—GENE RODDENBERRY

Let me tell you a story . . . and I will start at the end.

It was midmorning during a weekday in early November of 2020. I had just awoken when Geoff, my caregiver and friend, came into my room and told me that there was a package at the front door.

I asked him, "What is the package?"

He responded, "It's huge."

So I repeated, "What is it?"

A slight grin came across his face as he replied, "You'll see." Then, just as he started to turn away, he shouted over his shoulder, "I'll bring it around to the back."

I lay in my bed with anticipation, staring out the back door waiting. The moment Geoff entered the backyard with the package, a grand smile filled my face as I knew exactly what it was and whom it was from. It was a giant tree with a burlap root ball, ten feet high. But it wasn't just any tree . . . it was a tree from William Shatner.

Two weeks prior to this moment, Mr. Shatner had reached out and asked if I wanted to have a chat with him over Zoom. It's not every day The Captain makes such a generous offer, so I happily accepted. I had only had brief interactions with Bill before this, so I was very excited and curious about how our conversation would unfold. I imagined that we would talk about the current movies and TV shows that we each loved, his charity, or perhaps delve into some *Star Trek* lore. However, it turned out to be so much more than expected. In fact it ended up being one of the most meaningful and powerful conversations I have ever had. He was very curious about my upbringing in Canada, which we both have in common. He wanted to hear about my time at summer camp in Northern Ontario and my studies in landscape architecture at the University of Guelph. We spoke about our shared love of nature, and the connection we all share. The conversation led to his curiosity of my recent illness with ALS. I opened up to him, which flowed into a deep discussion about our personal mortality and what happens to us after we die. We were both very open and vulnerable, and it turned out that we share a similar philosophy about our transcendence into nature. I don't want to divulge all of the details, but I will let you know what he wrote on the card accompanying the package: "Dear Kenneth—Maybe YOU want to be a tree too. Thank you very much. Very fondly, Bill."

This tree, which now stands tall in my backyard, is more than just a beautiful memory of our conversation and shared love of nature. For me, the tree became a symbol of how gracious and special our *Star Trek* family is. I realize that we are two people with eight hundred episodes of *Star Trek* between us, yet here we are, connected and curious about each other. That is the beauty of *Star Trek*. Of course, it all begins with the writing, the characters, and their relationships displaying powerful themes of love, hope, discovery, inclusion, courage, curiosity, exploration, honor, sacrifice, service, diplomacy, trust, and science. However, I believe the essence of *Star Trek* goes beyond the material and transcends into our lives. This is the greatest gift that *Star Trek* gives us—how we connect with one another outside of the show. I am incredibly grateful for the friendships from my colleagues and the fans. I could tell you a magical story about each and every one of my cast mates and alumni or relate dozens of special interactions I've shared with the fans. We are a family, and I take great comfort in this unique phenomenon.

In dealing with my mortality, I feel comforted knowing that the characters I brought to life will live on. I'm blessed to have learned from them, the good and bad, and I'm proud of what they might offer others for years to come. However, the most precious benefit of being a part of *Star Trek* is the experience making it and all the people I have met along the way. The fabric of the *Star Trek* family is the true gift. Aside from sharing in characters, stories, and adventure, the common thread is each other. The special connection we have. This gives me the ultimate solace along my journey—the friendships and connections forged, knowing these memories will live on along with the characters.

Thank you for this gift.

And who knows, maybe some of you will one day breathe the oxygen from my leaves or lean on my trunk, which stands tall on the grounds of the new Starfleet Academy. Beside the ginkgo there will be a plaque that reads my favorite quote from Gene Roddenberry:

"In a very real sense, we are all aliens on a strange planet. We spend most of our lives reaching out and trying to communicate. If during our whole lifetime we could reach out and communicate with just two people, we are indeed very fortunate."

—KENNETH MITCHELL

Introduction

Starfleet is more than the central organizing force of the greatest pop culture franchises of all time. It is both the grounding and the motivating force behind many of *Star Trek*'s characters, stories, and epic moments. As the exploratory arm of the United Federation of Planets, itself made up of a disparate group of intergalactic species, it provides a framework under which they may all live together in the spirit of peace and prosperity. Similarly, *Star Trek* fandom, like Starfleet, is more than the sum of its parts. Though initially brought together by their shared love of *Star Trek*, people from all walks of life have united into a coalition that transcends age, gender, race, politics, or any other manufactured barrier to connection. By actively welcoming new people to share their love of *Star Trek*, fans are truly living the central tenets of Starfleet: "to seek out new life and new civilizations, to boldly go where no one has gone before." And it's their shared experience, their embracing of infinite diversity in infinite combinations, their commitment to support one another, that sets *Star Trek* fans apart from everyone else. More than a community, they—we—are a universal force of, and for, good. This book, spanning over fifty years of *Star Trek*, is a reminder of all that Starfleet—and *Star Trek* fandom—is and can be so that we can help each other live long and prosper.

—ROBB PEARLMAN

"They used to say if man could fly, he'd have wings . . . but he did fly. He discovered he had to. Do you wish that the first Apollo mission hadn't reached the moon, or that we hadn't gone on to Mars or the nearest star? . . . I'm in command. I could order this. But I'm not . . . because . . . Dr. McCoy is right in pointing out the enormous danger potential in any contact with life and intelligence as fantastically advanced as this. But I must point out that the possibilities, the potential for knowledge and advancement is equally great. Risk . . . risk is our business! That's what this starship is all about . . . that's why we're aboard her!"

—CAPTAIN JAMES T. KIRK

Starfleet is...

Forceful

Starfleet is...

Youth

Starfleet is... Experience

Starfleet is...

Trust

Starfleet is... Honor

Starfleet is...

Fun

Starfleet is...

Inclusive

Starfleet is...

Faithful

Starfleet is... Duty

Starfleet is...

Lawful

Starfleet is...

Illogical

Starfleet is...

Pioneering

Starfleet is... Elementary

"The first duty of every Starfleet officer is to tell the truth, whether it's scientific truth or historical truth or personal truth. It is the guiding principle on which Starfleet is based. And if you can't find it within yourself to stand up and tell the truth about what happened, you don't deserve to wear that uniform."

—CAPTAIN JEAN-LUC PICARD

Starfleet is...
Compassionate

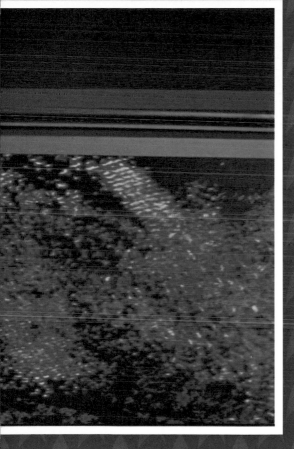

Starfleet is...

Amazing

Starfleet is...

Powerful

Starfleet is...

Empowered

Starfleet is...

Evolving

Starfleet is...

Communicative

Starfleet is...

Love

Starfleet is...

Education

Starfleet is...

Loyal

Starfleet is...

Exploration

Starfleet is...

Supportive

Starfleet is...

Changeable

Starfleet is...

Opportunity

Starfleet is...

Risk

Starfleet is... Decisive

"We are explorers. We explore our lives, day by day. And we explore the galaxy trying to expand the boundaries of our knowledge. And that is why I am here. Not to conquer you with weapons or ideas, but to coexist and learn."

—CAPTAIN BENJAMIN SISKO

Starfleet is...

Defiant

Starfleet is...

Redemptive

Starfleet is...

Defensive

Starfleet is... Empathetic

Starfleet is...

Sympathetic

Starfleet is...

Heartwarming

Starfleet is...

Heart-wrenching

Starfleet is...

Friendship

Starfleet is... Energized

Starfleet is... Protective

Starfleet is...

Hopeful

Starfleet is...

Animated

Starfleet is...
Generational

Starfleet is...

Forward-
thinking

"Starfleet is a promise. I give my life for you; you give your life for me. And nobody gets left behind."

—CAPTAIN CHRISTOPHER PIKE

Starfleet is...

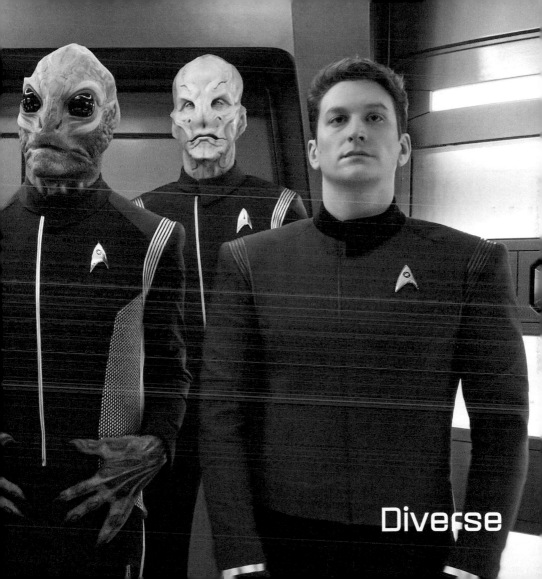

Diverse

Starfleet is...

Family

Starfleet is...

Sacrifice

Starfleet is...
Technology

Starfleet is...

Heartbreak

Starfleet is...

Solemn

Starfleet is...

Unshakable

Starfleet is...

Social

Starfleet is...

Celebratory

Starfleet is...

Romantic

"In a part of space where there are few rules, it's more important than ever that we hold fast to our own. In a region where shifting allegiances are commonplace, we have to have something stable to rely on. And we do . . . The principles and ideals of the Federation. As far as I'm concerned, those are the best allies we could have."

—CAPTAIN KATHERINE JANEWAY

Starfleet is...

Determination

Starfleet is...

Progress

Starfleet is...

Covert

Starfleet is...

Diplomatic

Starfleet is...

History

Starfleet is...

Solid

Starfleet is...

Curious

Starfleet is... Fallible

Starfleet is...

Encouraging

Starfleet is...

Transformative

Starfleet is...

Unique

Starfleet is...

Inventive

Starfleet is...

Understanding

Starfleet is...

Talent

Starfleet is...

Thoughtful

"Human beings have a code of behavior that applies whether they're Starfleet officers or space boomers, and it isn't driven by revenge. Just because someone isn't born on Earth doesn't make him any less human."

—CAPTAIN JONATHAN ARCHER

Starfleet is...

Enterprising

Starfleet is...

Experimental

Starfleet is...

Fearless

Starfleet is...

Measured

Starfleet is...

Yearning

Starfleet is...

Historic

Starfleet is...

Imaginative

Starfleet is...

Resistance

Starfleet is...

Awe-inspiring

Starfleet is...

Virtuous

StarFleet is... Nurturing

Starfleet is...

Inexplicable

StarFleet is... Unnatural

Starfleet is...

Surprising

"Some say that in life, there are no second chances. Experience tells me that this is true. But we can only look forward. We have to be torchbearers, casting the light so we may see our path to lasting peace. We will continue exploring, discovering new worlds, new civilizations. Yes—that is the United Federation of Planets . . . Yes—that is Starfleet . . . Yes, that is who we are . . . and who we will always be."

—CAPTAIN MICHAEL BURNHAM

Starfleet is...

Remote

Starfleet is...

Memory

Starfleet is...

Truth

Starfleet is...

Delicious

Starfleet is...

Tenacious

StarFleet is...

Prepared

Starfleet is...

Dogged

Starfleet is...

Rational

Starfleet is... Irrational

Starfleet is...

Ephemeral

Starfleet is...

Ethereal

Starfleet is...

Damaged

Starfleet is...

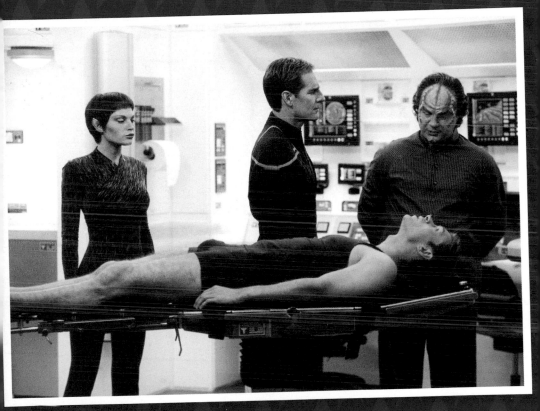

Resilient

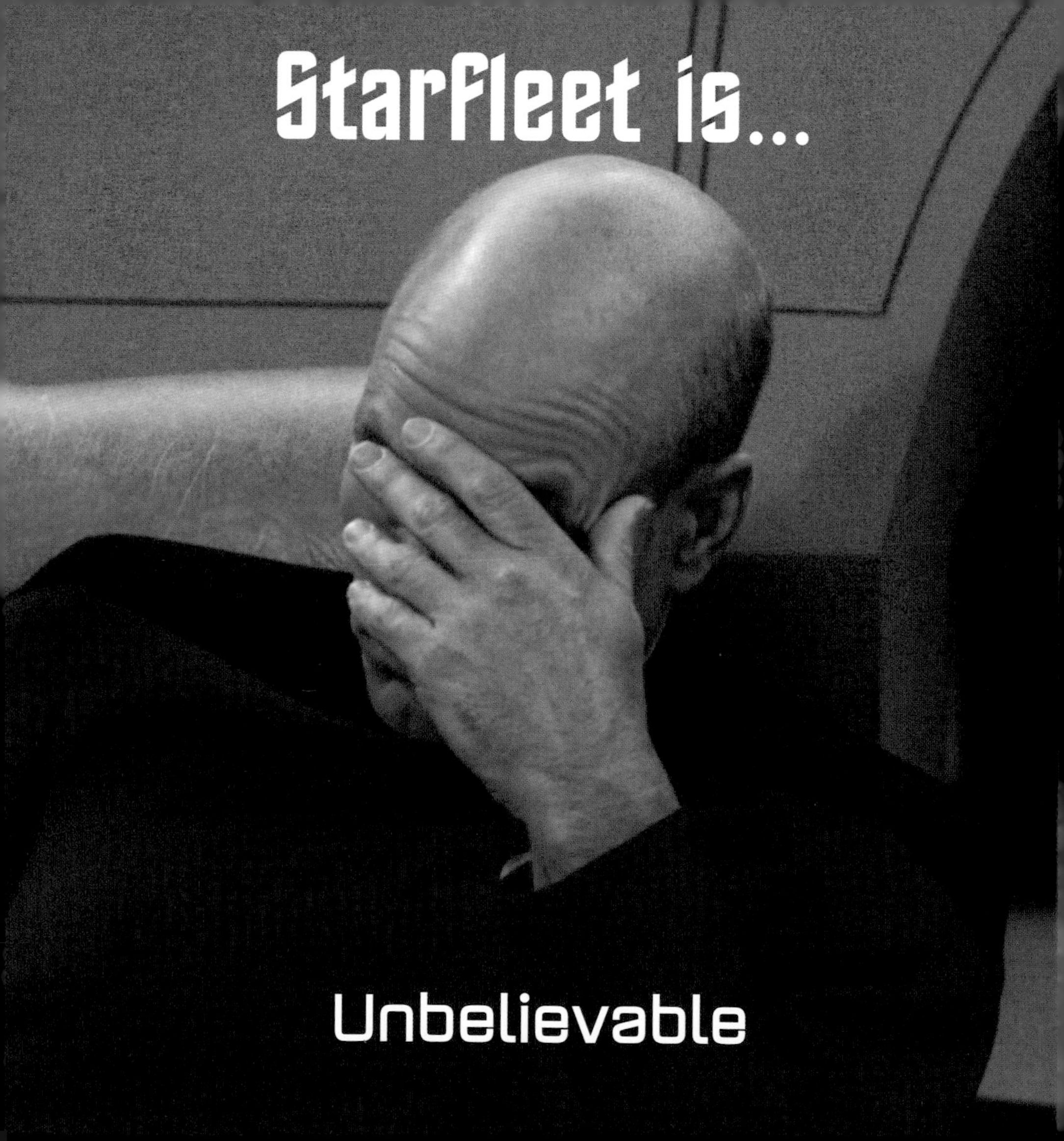
Starfleet is...
Unbelievable

Starfleet is...

Innovative

Starfleet is...

United

Starfleet is... Home

StarFleet is...

Nostalgic

Starfleet is... Timeless

"It is important to the typical *Star Trek* fan that there is a tomorrow. They pretty much share the *Star Trek* philosophies about life: the fact that it is wrong to interfere in the evolvement of other peoples, that to be different is not necessarily to be wrong or ugly."

—GENE RODDENBERRY